SAN ANTONIO
A PHOTOGRAPHIC FIESTA

PHOTOGRAPHY BY WERNER STEBNER
FOREWORD BY MAYOR LILA COCKRELL
AMERICAN GEOGRAPHIC PUBLISHING

I wish to thank my family for enduring the many hours I spent away from home, and also thank the many beautiful people I met in San Antonio.
To all, this book is a token of appreciation and love.

Front cover: The Alamo by night.
Back cover, top: A view of the city from the Durango Street Bridge over the San Antonio River.
Center: Kelly Air Force Base hosting the Air Force's Thunderbird team with their F-16s.
Bottom: The San Antonio River at Christmas.

ISBN 0-938314-94-7

© 1990 American Geographic Publishing
P.O. Box 5630, Helena, MT 59604
(406) 443-2842

William A. Cordingley, Chairman
Rick Graetz, President & CEO
Mark O. Thompson, Director of Publications
Barbara Fifer, Production Manager
Design by Linda Collins
Printed in Korea

American Geographic Publishing is a corporation for publishing illustrated geographic information and guides. It is not associated with American Geographical Society. It has no commercial or legal relationship to and should not be confused with any other company, society or group using the words geographic or geographical in its name or its publications.

Above: San Antonio cityscape as it greets visitors approaching the city.
Above left: Appropriately-named Mexican hat (ratibida columnaris) resembles the traditional high-crowned Mexican sombrero.
Title page: Fine detail of the legendary Rose Window at the San José Mission demonstrates the high craftsmanship of artisans who worked on the missions.

Werner Stebner, born in Germany, lives in Houston. He received a B.S. in mechanical engineering and metallurgy from Oregon State University. He regularly consults, lectures, researches and conducts workshops on photography and nature-related subjects, and has guided and photographed for expeditions in East Africa, Russia, the Galapagos Islands, China, Korea, Alaska, Spain and India. He has been given the General Electric Travel Photography Award and has won the Sierra Professional Photographers contest and the National Wildlife Photographers International Contest. His photography has appeared in books and various national periodicals.

FOREWORD

Everywhere you go in San Antonio, or in the pages of this book, you will find the brilliant colors of a unique community, generously blessed in the depth and richness of its cultural heritage.

The palette of cultural pigments from which San Antonio has been painted has many origins. Part explorer, part frontiersman. With roots drawn from early missionaries, nobility, settlers and ranchers, and later blended with Old and New World immigrants seeking freedom, bringing branches of nearly all of the Family of Man.

It's a canvas which is still being worked, as San Antonio today, embracing nearly a million people, continues to emerge as one of the Southwest's most promising urban centers.

Two hundred years after Columbus landed in the New World, another party of Spanish explorers charted the headwaters of a little spring-fed river of cool and clean water nestled in an abundant grove of cypress and pecan. The gushing springs gave them hope of future settlement, a promise that in the midst of the vast, sparsely vegetated lands they had traveled, this place would yield new life.

THEY NAMED THE RIVER San Antonio de Padua in honor of St. Anthony, whose feast day (June 13) it was, although the stream already had another, descriptive native name, Yanaguana ("Drunken Old Man Going Home at Night"), which aptly portrayed its twisting, curving course.

It would be nearly another 20 years before settlement began. In 1718, Spanish military officials and missionaries arrived to prepare the first of what would be a chain of forts and missions north of the Río Grande, a combined force of "cross and sword" to civilize the frontier, and keep it from the hands of rival French interests.

They founded San Antonio de Valero, later renamed San Antonio del Alamo. In swift order, other missions followed: San Jose with its distinctive dome and ornate Rose Window, Concepción, Espada, and San Juan Capistrano.

With the missions came colonists, several hundred settlers from the Canary Islands and from throughout the new Spanish empire, and the establishment of a presidio of troops to guard against raiding Comanches and Lipan Apaches and the threat of other European powers.

Above: Artistry of door handles at Mission San Juan.

Facing page: The entrance to the Alamo chapel, one of the most-visited historical monuments in Texas.

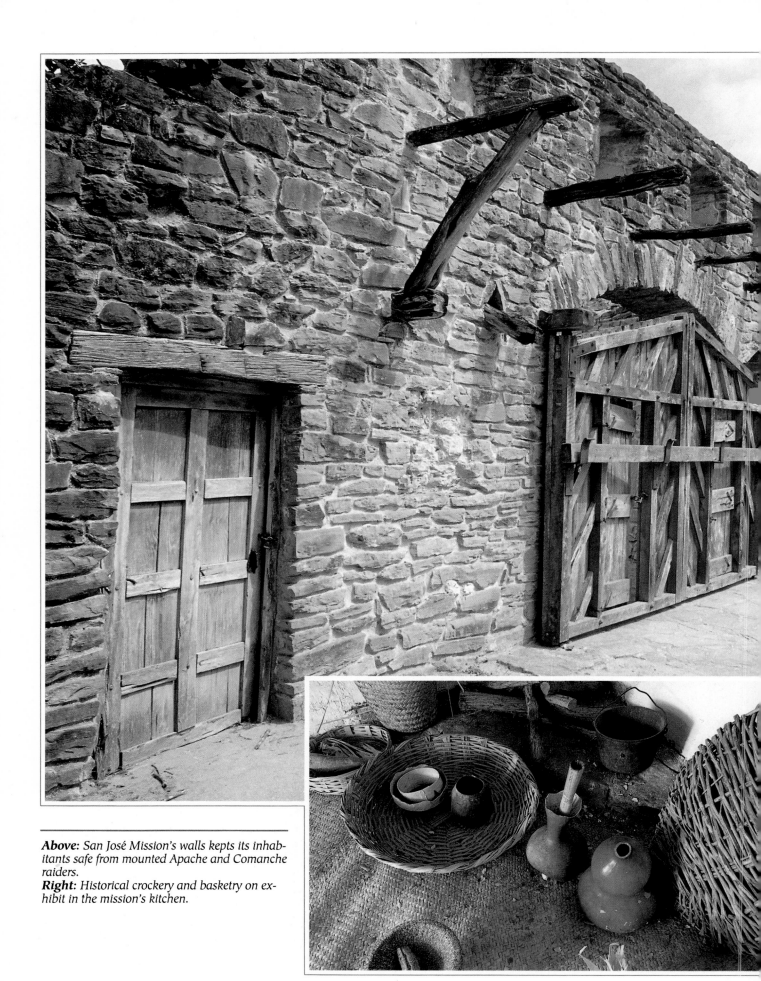

Above: San José Mission's walls kepts its inhabitants safe from mounted Apache and Comanche raiders.
Right: Historical crockery and basketry on exhibit in the mission's kitchen.

They laid out their plan for the Villa de Bexar, including the appropriate squares which would be the centers of the village. They dug a system of acequias to water their fields, and attempted to bring religion, agriculture and industry to the indigenous Coahuiltecan natives. There matters stood for the rest of the century, with little change except for the gradual growth of commerce along the Camino Real, the trail linking Spain's outposts on the frontier.

The architecture and artifacts of this period are abundantly preserved throughout San Antonio, from the missions, Espada Aqueduct and La Villita with its thick-walled haciendas to the Spanish Governor's Palace and the oldest public park in the West at San Pedro Springs. Preserved too are the memory of many of the early families in the place names of our city: Navarro, Veramendi, Yturri among many.

THE EARLY SPANISH AND MEXICAN influence also flavors the celebrations of our community. The event-packed days of Fiesta in April bring parades along streets and waterways, entertainment to meet a variety of tastes, and the excitement of "Night in Old San Antonio." Cinco de Mayo (May 5) and Diez y Seis (September 16) celebrate battles for freedom in Mexico. In December, the Fiesta de Las Luminarias turns the Riverwalk into a shimmering, candle-lit venue for the procession of Las Posadas, the Search for the Inn.

The Hispanic legacy goes deep. Language, food, culture and customs. In San Antonio, as perhaps in no other North American city, Hispanic ways intertwined with the westward push of English-speaking and Western European migration. Freedom-seeking emigrés from England, Ireland, Germany and France came, knowing that land ownership and their skills could secure the liberty they sought.

Freedom's beacon flashed continuously in San Antonio's history, as wave after wave of revolutions swept south of the Río Grande, forcing thousands to flee in their wakes.

Many took refuge in San Antonio. Some returned to their home countries after brief exile. Others stayed, finding new ventures and enterprises, contributing a passion for democratic values to the city's political ethos, a heritage that remains today.

With the opening of the West, a new thread of San Antonio's history began to be spun.

English-speaking settlers with legendary names like Austin, Bowie and Houston began to trek west to the fertile river valleys west of the Louisiana Territory. Enterprising and robust, they soon dominated

Above: Street signs near the Alamo honor two of its defenders.

Facing page, top: Mission Espada. Its arched doorway has generated much speculation. Some think it was a mistake, while others find beauty in its inversion.
Bottom: Side entrance of the Alamo.

the population and called themselves Texians.

Spirited forward by democratic ideals, the newcomers soon rebelled against the distant, but iron-fisted, authority of the newly established nation of Mexico, and events quickly led to the hastily fortified walls of the abandoned mission known as del Alamo.

IN THE WINTER OF **1836,** the call for a defense of San Antonio carried throughout the Texas landscape. By February, nearly 200 Texian and Mexican colonists had gathered inside the old mission. Outside, thousands of troops under the command of General Santa Anna, weary and cold from their forced march across the brushy plains, began the siege that would last 13 days.

On March 6 the small garrison was overrun and all 188 defenders put to death. The few women and children who had remained with the heroic volunteers were left to mourn.

Through their sacrifice, however, Santa Anna's advance was slowed, allowing the Texians under Sam Houston to assemble a force adequate to drive the general's troops back into Mexico. Several weeks after the fall of the Alamo, the Mexicans were stopped at San Jacinto. A new nation—Texas—and a new rallying cry—"Remember the Alamo!"—were born.

SAN ANTONIO TODAY remembers the Alamo. It's our nickname, "Alamo City," our landmark symbol, replicated in architecture and facades throughout the city, and the gathering place for many community events.

It's also a hallowed shrine of liberty. Inside its massive wooden doors, the story of those 13 Days of Glory are enshrined in exhibits and artifacts. A cenotaph on Alamo Plaza memorializes the Alamo's heroes: Crockett, Bowie, Travis, Smith, Bonham, Esparza and others. In the peaceful gardens surrounding the chapel are other memo-

rials, including one given by the Japanese in honor of a similar event in their history.

The Alamo is also a center of inspiration to future heroes of our country, as thousands of military personnel train and serve within San Antonio. Five major military bases and more than 80,000 uniformed personnel call San Antonio home.

These bases include Lackland Air Force Base, the basic training center for the Air Force; Kelly Air Force Base, site of a logistics center handling everything from C-5As and B-52s to nuclear weapons; Randolph Air Force Base and its pilot training center; and Brooks Air Force Base, home to the School of Aerospace Medicine.

THE ARMY'S MAJOR medical training site, the Academy of Health Sciences, and Brooke Army Hospital are located at Fort Sam Houston. "Fort Sam" began as the forward command of the string of forts that guarded the southern westward routes to California. Here Geronimo and his conquered Apache chiefs were imprisoned and troops were raised to pursue Pancho Villa into Mexico. It was along Fort Sam Houston's parade field that U.S. military aviation was launched in the flight of a Wright Brothers-constructed aircraft.

Each of these facilities has public exhibits allowing visitors to trace military events from the days of western expansion and frontier service to the Space Age. Many displays memorialize those famous military leaders who served here and then went on to greater fame: Robert E. Lee, Dwight D. Eisenhower, "Black Jack" Pershing, Theodore Roosevelt (who recruited Rough Riders among the able horsemen of San Antonio and South Texas), and aviators Hap Arnold and Billy Mitchell.

Cattle, oil and commerce dominated San Antonio's transition into the Twentieth Century. The first of the great cattle drives north into Kansas and beyond was organized in and around San Antonio.

Barbed wire, which would change the face of the West forever, was first demonstrated in the streets of San Antonio and one famous local family lent its name to particularly ornery dogies, which became known as "mavericks."

Today, those industries, although still important, have been joined by ventures undreamed of by the first San Antonians. Backed by a wealth of educational and research institutions, San Antonio is a key

Above: The Taj Mahal, a National Historic Monument, at Randolph Air Force Base.

Facing page: Kelly Air Force Base is a major B-52 and C-5A maintenance facility. Here, a C-5A tail provides welcome shade for visitors.

Above: *Paseo del Río: the San Antonio River winds its way through downtown, carrying barges that offer formal meals.*

Facing page: *Food and fun: synonymous with the city.*

center for biotechnical and engineering advances. The frontier of the West has been replaced by a frontier of knowledge leading to unforeseen contributions to our well-being.

And it's little wonder that tourism has become an important sector of the city's life. Blessed with a mild climate and numerous attractions, San Antonio has become one of the country's premier tourist centers.

IN 1968 SAN ANTONIO hosted HemisFair. This world-class event left a legacy both of facilities and of renewed interest in San Antonio's unique Riverwalk area. From the 750-foot tall Tower of the Americas to convention, sports and performing arts facilities and new hotels, restaurants and stores, downtown San Antonio has been the site of increased public and private investment to serve visitors, including a new, 65,000-seat, indoor stadium—the AlamoDome.

Strolling along the Riverwalk is a must, where you can sample entertaining sounds and tasty flavors from half a dozen cultures. The Riverwalk is also home to numerous celebrations and festivals throughout the year and its cypress-lined banks evoke a special, park-like experience, whether visited on foot or on a relaxed river barge ride.

Tourist interest isn't restricted to the downtown. From a first-class zoological park and botanical gardens, to art and history museums, shopping, dining and entertainment, anywhere you turn the city has something exciting to offer. Our newest additions include Sea World of Texas and Fiesta Texas.

The internationally-renowned San Antonio Festival, Stockshow and Rodeo, grand prix racing, Fiesta, and professional sports led by our NBA stalwarts, the San Antonio Spurs, highlight a fun-packed entertainment calendar.

San Antonians have a special pride in their richly deserved recognition as an All-America City, and a quick friendliness that lives up to a Native American word for friend, "tejas," which gave the state its name. The character of our people, and the collision of cultures that met in San Antonio and left a flavor and ambiance found nowhere else, form a lasting claim to the word "unique." I hope the colors of this collection of photographs will provide you with a sense of both our culture and our pride.

—*Mayor Lila Cockrell*

Above: Common egret (casmerodius albus) *in mating plumage.*
Right: A quiet, peaceful view of the Riverwalk in "Host City, USA."

TRAVIS   CROCKETT

SEPH KERR · GEORGE C. KIMBLE · WILLIAM P. KING · JOHN G. KING · WILLIAM IRVINE LEWIS · WILLIAM J. LIGHTFOOT · JONATHAN
BERT McKINNEY · ELIEL MELTON · THOMAS R. MILLER · WILLIAM MILLS · ISAAC MILLSAPS · EDWARD F. MITCHASSON · EDWI
ANTONIO PADILLO · WILLIAM PARKS · RICHARDSON PERRY · AMOS POLLARI

Above: *This marble cenotaph commemorates the soldiers of the Republic of Texas who defended the Alamo, 188 of whom were killed after a 13-day siege.*
Left: *The All-America City is a continuous ambassador to the world.*

Facing page: *Memories of gunslingers during Fiesta.*

Left: *The Air Force Thunderbird team, visiting from their home of Nellis Air Force Base, Nevada, take part in San Antonio's Armed Forces Appreciation Day 1990.*

Below: *Major Chuck Greenwood, Pilot Number 5 and lead solo of the Thunderbirds in 1990, with his F-16 fighter.*

Above: The Liberty Bar in the old Boehlers Beer Garden provides really down-home Texas cooking. A must: mesquite-grilled steak.
Right: Tex-Mex is both traditional local food and favored local dress.

Facing page: Modern art at the Groos Bank building on the 410 loop.

Above: *A San Antonio smile welcomes all.*
Left: *Cowboy skills at work within sight of the modern city.*

Right: Several species of Texas bluebonnets blanket large areas of the state in spring. All are designated the official state flower; pictured here is lupinus texenis.
Below: Store-sign cowboy waits for the moon to set.

Above: *The red-tailed hawk* (buteo jamaicensis) *hunts in open country, brush or woodlands.*
Right: *San Antonio is surrounded by varied landscapes. The dry climate and heat create a home for rattlesnakes.*

Facing page: *The gates of Hemis-Fair Park, with the Marriott Hotel beyond.*

The Riverwalk and downtown viewed from the Marriott Hotel.

Right: Blue jay (cyanocitta cristata) is native to Texas.
Below: Fresh lemonade at the Mercado can help cool the summer days.

Facing page: Cactus at the San Antonio Botanical Center, located at 555 Funston Place, where one can enjoy an intriguing blend of flora and architecture.

Above: *San Antonio's Municipal Building in the foreground, shadowed by the walls of the Southwestern Bell Telephone Building.*

Facing page: *The San Antonio* Light *newspaper building.*

Above: *One of Sea World's walruses. These bewhiskered comedians try to solve the mystery of Uncle Schmedley's will in the Spooky, Kooky Castle Show.™*
Left: *Sea World's Shamu performing in the world's largest marine mammal habitat.*

Above: A lone Texas oak views the sunset.

Left: Artist in glass, located in La Villita. This area, nestled in the shadows of luxury hotels, across the street from the bustling HemisFair Plaza, is the historic heart of the city, with charmingly restored adobe shops and galleries.

Facing page: Arneson River Theatre, where the river is as much a part of the performance as the bill—which ranges from mariachis to flamenco, opera to country western.

Above: *The favorite wedding photography setting, the McNay Art Museum at 6000 North New Braunsfels Avenue, is housed within an Andalusian-inspired mansion designed by San Antonio architects Atlee B. and Robert Ayres.*
Right: *Whether you call it Indian blanket or firewheel, this flower (gaillardia) blooms from April to June, blanketing fields that then resemble the bright tapestries of the western Indians.*

Above: *San Antonio offers variety in shopping.*
Left: *A shoeshine and an update on local gossip at Mercado Square.*

Facing page: *Detail of the Southwestern Bell Telephone Building. San Antonio is a showcase of architectural styles.*

Sharing a western sunset.

Looking down from the Tower of the Americas, with the modern Convention Center in foreground.

At the San Antonio Zoo, Brackenridge Park:
Above: A cheetah, the world's fastest cat, rests at sunset.
Right: Flamingo.
Facing page: This giant panda also is a San Antonian.

Above: Building for another Fiesta. San Antonio has spent millions on new highways, hotels and other tourist facilities.
Right: Tower of the Americas—750 feet tall—at the site of the 1968 World's Fair.

Above: San Antonio Botanical Center's 38-acre garden represents, in miniature, the many landscapes of Texas.
Left: World-class jazz in San Antonio at The Landing, home of the great jazz performers.

Facing page: San Antonio shows off its diverse cultural heritage during Fiesta.

Above: *The blue grosbeak (guiraca caerulea) is a summer resident to be seen in thickets and brushy places, and along roadsides.*
Right: *Bluebells (eustoma grandiflorum)—one of the loveliest of Texas wild flowers.*

Above: *Fajitas, a San Antonio trademark.*

Facing page: *The lighted top of the Tower Life Building, San Antonio's first true skyscraper.*

Above: "Don't Mess with Texas" was a successful anti-littering campaign's slogan **Left:** Preparing for an early-morning flight.

Above: St. Peter-St. Joseph Children's Home is a fine example of the architectural influence of the missions.
Right: Hand-crafted door and opener at Mission San José.

Facing page: San José Mission, viewed as the model among Texas missions.

Above: San Antonio accommodates many lifestyles and nationalities. This Filipina woman is traditionally dressed for the International Festival in June.
Left: Interior of San Fernando cathedral. Having celebrated its 250th anniversary in 1989, it is the oldest cathedral sanctuary in the United States.

Above: Water fun at Sea World, where daredevil skiers perform Beach Blanket Ski Party™ on a 12-acre lake.
Left: Splashtown USA on I-35 North compares favorably with a beachfront park.

Facing page: During Fiesta, Mercado streets become informal dance saloons.

A morning view of the river and the downtown area.

Above: *This male African lion, a popular attraction at the San Antonio Zoo, is a little worse for the wear following a domestic dispute.*
Right: *Buttercups (oenothera serrucata), with their delicate petals, usually open in the afternoon, then wither the next day.*

Above: *Splashtown USA—combine 2 million gallons of crystal-clear water and lots of people, and you have instant family fun.*

Facing page: *A caretaker in the King William district pauses for a breather.*

Left: The essence of San Antonio's enchantment can be captured during a stroll along the Riverwalk, seen here in Christmas decor.
Below: European-style outdoor cafes provide food and rest.

Above: *Early morning fog swathes a ranch outside the city.*
Left: *A plains prickly pear cactus.*

Facing page: *Texas bluebonnets decorate an old pioneer settlement.*

Above: *The Mercado, located between West Commerce and Dolorosa, provides an escape south of the Border, with its sidewalk cafes and sidewalk artists galore.*

Facing page: *A summer walk along the San Antonio River. The River Architecture Committee controls construction in order to allow a natural vegetation to grow.*

Overleaf: *San Antonio's modern hotels stand ready to serve. Shown is the Marriott Hotel.*

Above: Hoops!
Right: Millions of convention-goers and tourists enjoy barge trips along the San Antonio River each year.

Above: *This Louisiana heron* (hydranassa tricolor), *sometimes called a tricolor heron, is looking for a meal near the Mission Aquaduct.*

Facing page, top: *"Madame Butterfly," performed at the Sunken Garden in Brackenridge Park during the San Antonio Festival.*
Bottom: *Claret cup cactus* (echinocereus triglochidiatus) *is one of several hundred cactus species indigenous to Texas. It blooms in early spring and then periodically until late fall, especially following rainstorms.*

Above: The Taj Mahal, a Randolph Air Force Base landmark, is the base's water tower. In the foreground stands the "missing man formation" monument to pilots Missing In Action.
Left: The younger generation extends a San Antonio welcome.

Facing page: Early morning mist on a homestead near the city.

Above: *A roseate spoonbill (ajaia agaga) rests at sunset in the San Antonio River.*
Left: *The Riverwalk at sunset.*

Above: *Texans are proud of both their cars and their horses. Here two types of beautiful horse-power fortuitously came together for the camera.*

Facing page, top: *The parade field at Fort Sam Houston, surrounded by Brooke Army Medical Center.*
Bottom: *St. Mary's University was founded in 1852.*

Above: *Military macaws at Sea World, which boasts colorful avian exhibits.*

Facing page: *White fleabane and purple wine cup join with Indian blanket in a springtime mosaic.*

Overleaf: *Mariachis provide entertainment at a poolside party during San Antonio's Fiesta in April.*